Wild Flight

6/24/23

For Deborah,
On a beautiful
day in St. Clair Shores —
With all best wishes,
Christine

The Walt McDonald
First-Book Series in Poetry

Robert A. Fink, *editor*

Wild Flight

CHRISTINE RHEIN
Introduction by Robert A. Fink

Christine Rhein

Texas Tech
University Press

This book is typeset in Filosofia. The paper used in this book meets the
minimum requirements of ANSI/NISO Z39.48-1992 (R1997). ∞

Designed by Lindsay Starr

LIBRARY OF CONGRESS CATALOGING-IN-PUBLICATION DATA
Rhein, Christine.
     Wild flight / Christine Rhein ; introduction by Robert A. Fink.
     p. cm.—(The Walt McDonald first-book series in poetry)
Summary: "The 2007 winner of the Walt McDonald First-Book Series in
Poetry, this collection explores a range of "flights," from the working world of
Detroit to American suburbia and pop culture; from the European landscape
of World War II to the current war in Iraq"—Provided by publisher.
     ISBN-13: 978-0-89672-621-5 (hardcover: alk. paper)
     ISBN-10: 0-89672-621-5 (hardcover: alk. paper)
     I. Title.
PS3618.H45W55 2008
811'.6—dc22   2007029426

PRINTED IN THE UNITED STATES OF AMERICA
09 10 11 12 13 14 15 16 17 / 9 8 7 6 5 4 3 2 1

ISBN-13: 978-0-89672-667-3
First paperback printing, 2009

TEXAS TECH UNIVERSITY PRESS
Box 41037, Lubbock, Texas 79409-1037 USA
800.832.4042 | ttup@ttu.edu | www.ttup.ttu.edu

For my parents, Horst and Eleonore Misch,
and for my sister, Tammy Misch Wilms

ACKNOWLEDGMENTS

Grateful acknowledgment is made to the editors of the following journals where these poems first appeared, some in slightly different versions:

Alligator Juniper: "Before the Word *Depression*"
Americas Review: "During Plans for War, Crows—"
Atlanta Review: "Poem in February"
Crab Orchard Review: "My Father Talks of 1946"
Driftwood Review: "Exercising to Poetry Videos," "How to Tell It"
The Gettysburg Review: "'Another Good Kid Shot Dead in Detroit'," "Not Another," "On Art," "Our Twenty-First Summer, Chimney Swifts," "To the Previous Owner"
The MacGuffin: "Flight Path," "For My Son, at Twelve," "Girl in the Photograph," "In the Morning Paper," "Wren's Nest in a Saguaro"
Margie: "Artiste Maurice Bennett Explains His 'Burning Desire'," "In the Women's Room," "This Winter"
Michigan Quarterly Review: "One of those questions"
Pavement Saw: "In Detroit, circa 1970," "Night Poem"
The Southern Review: "In Code," "Upon Being Asked What I Believe In," "Waiting"
Sow's Ear Poetry Review: "Story Problems"

"One of those questions" was awarded the *Michigan Quarterly Review* 2006 Laurence Goldstein Poetry Prize and was included in *Best New Poets 2007.*

"Not Another" was featured at *Poetry Daily* on December 20, 2006.

"Artiste Maurice Bennett Explains His 'Burning Desire'" appeared in the anthology *Mona Poetica*.

I also gratefully acknowledge the support I received through a 2002 writers' conference scholarship from AWP and a 2004 individual artist grant from the Barbara Deming Memorial Fund.

A mechanical engineer doesn't become a poet without a great deal of help. I extend heartfelt thanks to friends and mentors in Detroit, Ann Arbor, and beyond for guiding my journey and contributing to this book in various, wonderful ways. I am especially grateful to the Springfed Arts community, to all the poets—past and present—in the Tuesday night workshop, and to our teacher-extraordinaire, Mary Jo Firth Gillett. This collection would not have been possible without Mary Jo, who helped improve every poem with kind nudging, generous care, and much wisdom. I am indebted to Robert Fink, Judith Keeling, and the entire staff at Texas Tech University Press. My deepest gratitude, as always, goes to my husband, Chuck, and our sons, Rob and Jamie, for making the "flight" we share a perfectly wild and joyous ride.

CONTENTS

INTRODUCTION

When asked, "What do you believe in?," how many poets could answer, "the pulse / of algebra, all those x's busy intersecting / all those y's, points aligned," then add "the tangle of science and poetry," then, almost as an afterthought, sharp turn of "the tunneling mind," throw in "the wild flight of fireflies, bodies glowing / from both desire and defense" ("Upon Being Asked What I Believe In")? I'm thinking only a Detroit, automotive-industry, mechanical-engineer, Romantic-Realist poet reconciling opposites into paradoxes defining the joy of order and abandon, a wild, erratic flight of "sudden stalls, startling speed," weaving patterns we can and cannot figure out ("Our Twenty-First Summer, Chimney Swifts"), could answer the question so as to celebrate both harnessed energy and its climactic release.

Christine Rhein's first collection of poems is happily titled *Wild Flight*: joyful celebration of a flight path both filed and improvised, cautious pattern and heedless fun set against a skyline of war and displacement, a land of rubble, both historical and all too present, where *wild* qualifies *flight* as *panic* and *nightmare*—"the unknown that part of us / is waiting for" ("Waiting") and also as the nonchalance of swifts, "silhouette of tiny arrow / and wide-reaching bow," avian acrobats living mostly in the air ("Our Twenty-First Summer, Chimney Swifts"). Here is flight as language defining the creative tension between engineer—her "calculated quest for / a certain and safe design," and poet—filling her "notebook lines / she is bound to ignore" ("Self-Portraits, Three-Way Mirror").

There is no neat way to introduce this book. It has taken me four hours and twenty minutes in the Saturday silence of my university office to draft two paragraphs. *Wild Flight* will not permit any attempt at a reductive interpretation of metaphor and thematic motif. The beauty and order of this collection is both that of Fibonacci's mathematical sequence, "the pattern obeyed by sunflower petals, pine cone whorls" ("Story Problems"), and improvisation "with ingredients at hand" ("Upon Being Asked What I Believe In"). It is *Pantoum* and free-flight interior monologue, stream of haunting memory. It is what Annie Dillard wrote of Dave Rahm, stunt pilot—"the air's own genius" flying his black Bücker Jungman plane, carving "the air into forms that built wildly and musically on each other and never ended," smattering "the sky with landscapes and systems" (*The Writing Life*, Harper Perennial, 1989, p. 95).

You've heard this before: "I started reading and couldn't put it down." With Chris Rhein's manuscript, not only could I not put it down, I feared turning each page, almost certain the pilot could not sustain such blood-rushing combinations, such patterns and deviations, and return whole to earth, touch down, roar off into another poem. When the ride ended, I got in line to go again.

This introduction doesn't even come close to conveying the rush I felt in flight. Already it reads to me as if Neil Armstrong, being asked to explain his first-man-on-the-moon experience, had replied, "We went up there and walked around and came back home." Reading, studying, *Wild Flight* is one of those experiences you have to know first hand, and then your response may be that of the hush that swells through the audience following the final note of the Brahms *Requiem*, the Beethoven *Fifth Symphony*, prelude to explosive release, standing-ovation applause.

Wild Flight maneuvers us through five levels of air, a symphony of carefully orchestrated memory—the need to witness: "to name the dance / *efficient, elegant,* the wren's flight *brave*" ("Wren's Nest in a Saguaro"), the wren in this symphony being the poet-persona Chris Rhein and also her father, her mother, her sister, her grandparents, Chris's husband, their sons, even you and I, and our neighbors— those world-wide, next-door strangers, the seeming enemies Jesus instructed his followers to love as themselves. *We* are the personae of this book—common folk displaying uncommon valor.

The book's five sections engage us in our song of self, song of home, moving from our anger and despair at displacement in war to the recognition and hope of beauty even in the midst of yet another war. Even as we sing with Chris Rhein, our song soaring with the swifts, nesting with the wren "flying in / and out of spikes, feathers grazing barbs" of the cactus, creating "a home / amid giant thorns," we do not ignore the loss and guilt we know too well ("Wren's Nest in a Saguaro").

Section I introduces the poet-persona's father, "born on the wrong side" of the Oder River ("My Father's *Geschichte*"), his child-hood and youth in Silesia before, during, and after World War II. Displaced from his home, his homeland, to Czechoslovakia, he became a *"Flüchtling*—the word for refugee" ("My Father Talks of 1946")—then walked back to Polish-controlled Silesia, displaced now *in* his home. It is this historical and personal displacement that sets up one of the central motifs of the collection—the loss of *home-land*, "who goes, who stays" ("Story Problems")—the desire to go home, and the sacrifice and courage required to prevail in a world transformed by "bullet after unwitting bullet" ("Gift").

The first section also introduces the quest of the poet-persona to know her father's story, to identify with her father and other dis-placed individuals, a witness to their lives of innocence, sacrifice, and heroism—protecting, feeding their families, believing in the beauty and order of nature to heal, regenerate, her father choosing for his lifelong trade the art and sweat of reconstructing home and family: "Bricklaying seemed like a good idea / in a land of rubble" ("My Father Talks of 1946").

Section II focuses on Christine Rhein, poet-persona, desiring to know herself though her paradoxical self portrait as engineer and poet, a product of Detroit—her Silesia—but nothing like her father's displaced homeland. She attempts to block out fears of the "shadows of *chance* and *fate*" ("How to Tell It") by pretending to be the beau-tiful, good witch Samantha and the hero climbing "the giant rope in Gym," not the weak girl "stuck," clinging to the rope ("In Detroit, circa 1970"). She pumps iron, crunching through sit-ups, training to live life by writing about it ("Exercising to Poetry Videos"), but she cannot escape imagining herself *victim*, identifying with an international cast of family: Mohammed Sesay mutilated in Sierra

Leone; an Indian girl whom Chris wants to "feed . . . soup and cake, / bathe . . . , tuck . . . into bed" ("Girl in the Photograph"); a Detroit mother whose little girl is shot dead on her porch; Janet Leigh, the actress stabbing victim in Hitchcock's *Psycho*, whose "life changed by pretending," leaving the actress, like Chris Rhein, like all of us, "*vulnerable*" ("Waiting").

Section III begins the transition from *flight* to *nesting*, building a nest, a shelter for the poet-persona's young: "Not art but necessity / creates a home / amid giant thorns" ("Wren's Nest in a Saguaro"). The poet-persona returns both figuratively and literally to the street of her youth wondering what she might be looking for ("At Sway"). She returns as well to the stories of her parents' history—how they came together, having escaped a world of uniforms and ultimatums to build a home for their two daughters in Detroit, an ending her father could not believe would be *happy*; rather, he sought "to be *content*" ("We were four—"). His daughter, now married and a mother sitting up nights, the radio's Motown warning, "*No where to run, / no where to hide*" ("Night Poem"), worries about time running out, the necessity of letting go of her sons, her parents. She types a line, the emotion earnest, grief unhidden.

Section IV: In the midst of the noise of war, the clichés of empty rhetoric, and the persona-poet's sometime wish to flee from so many responsibilities, the beat, the humor, of life (some noise, some music) is heard as *heartbeat*; and the daughter of refugees settles down with husband, sons, and friends. Comfortable in her heavy, wingless coat ("One of those questions"), she settles for luck, for joy, for love—"the swoosh, the quiver" of her husband's breath as he kisses her ear, whispers her name ("Tuning").

Section V concludes *Wild Flight* by celebrating what is gained through the struggle to locate our true home, our homeland. Through displacement and suffering, the outcasts of the world can find healing by means of acceptance of our rightful place at the table set for all in the house of humanity, the house that is our "very person" (epigraph to Section V). Wherever we fly, we carry home within us. We *are* our homeland. "Flight Path" opens Section V reiterating our sense of displacement, our desire to go home, then celebrates our family of humans, our prayer for peace, our hope for our children—a flight path from war-torn, "overcast" point *A* to the "definite" point

B toward which each of us is destined, nothing we *"can do but pray"* for the future of our world family: "Let *B* be the place called making a baby happy" ("Flight Path"). When asked what she believes in, the poet-persona can now reply: "the days I'm sunk / *in* up to my waist, improvising / with ingredients at hand"; her "babies' / milk-drunk faces"; her "teenage sons"; her "husband offering / to warm my feet"; and finally, the paradoxical "wild / flight of fireflies, bodies glowing / from both desire and defense" ("Upon Being Asked What I Believe In").

And because she has reconciled *engineer* and *poet* in answering the call of her father to someday have *"a writer in the family again,"* the poet-persona can declare, "How little, really, we decide in life, how wild the impact, / what gets learned by heart" ("Washing Windows"). What she has learned is that "love, too, is art, / because we crave its thrill, / emotion swooping down on wings" ("On Art"). *Love* and *home* are as simple, as complex, as a wife and her husband settled in their "living room": "Your hand in mine, / we talk of our sons / growing older," and like the endangered chimney swifts, who "live mostly in the air," the couple can now, as night "allows some rest," clamp clawed feet side by side on the chimney's "firebricks with mortared joints"—a cozy, precarious nesting, "a cliff wall to cling to" ("Our Twenty-First Summer, Chimney Swifts").

The final poem, "Not Another," reconciles the book's paradoxical motifs. The bullet is still being fired; families are still displaced, but even in Iraq with its daily bombings, its rocket and mortar attacks, a U. S. soldier records in his web log a wood pigeon's sitting on her nest while other pigeons power up then swoop down *"almost like they're doing it for fun."* Birds sing, the poet-persona learns from the author of *Why Birds Sing*, because "'they must, . . . and because they love to.'" She can now acknowledge that our life, our art, is "the work of weaving." We do what we can. Like the soldier, like the poet-persona, we choose to take hope near *"an amphitheater from Alexander the Great's time"* as we record our ironic, first sighting of the *"laughing dove."*

Robert A. Fink ABILENE, 2008

My travel agents were Hitler and Stalin.

CHARLES SIMIC

1944, a German boy walks home
from school, Russian POWs working
in the park. *Brot, Brot,* one of them
whispers with a strange accent, hungry
eyes. The next day the boy saves
the butter sandwich that is his lunch,
tries to hand it to the prisoner who shakes
his head, looks up at the guard
on the bridge, and willing the blade
of his shovel into frozen ground,
cocks his head toward a nearby tree.

Sixty years later, my father and I
stand in the same spot—the bridge
so close, the guard must have seen,
looked away—and my father isn't sure
how many times he placed his bread,
wrapped in old headlines, behind
the tree—grown huge now—or whether,
on that afternoon when he found a toy,
a little wooden gun, propped against
the trunk, the workers were still there.

I like to think the Russian saw
my father smile, that he lived
to carve another make-believe
pistol, to watch his son fit
a rubber band into the careful groove,
around the bent nail trigger, and just
as the German boy had, aim freely
into the air, firing pebbles or bits
of twig, bullet after unwitting bullet.

My Father's *Geschichte*

die Geschichte means
both *story* and *history*

I.

He says the nightmares stopped sometime
in his forties, the ones I witnessed in childhood
when he napped on the couch, shouting

himself awake—January 1945 all over again,
the run from Russian troops moving west,
burning homes, raping women—and always

the same dream: his mother hidden while he
stood lookout, his body pressed against the door,
soldiers laughing, pushing from the other side.

At seventy, he nearly chuckles at the long-lived fear,
the way he does when his accent prompts
someone to ask where in Germany he's from

and he begins: *I'm not sure how much you know
about history. Have you heard of the Oder River?
Well, I was born on the wrong side of it . . .*

II.

A child, I loved the story of that winter
escape, the adventure of a whole village—
just a day ahead of the Russians—fleeing
on foot, pulling horses and carts through snow,
my father sometimes sent ahead to find a barn,
some shelter for the coming night,
a place to cook the turkey and rabbits
he had hurriedly butchered before they left,

the turkey running headless in the moonlit yard.
I couldn't feel the bitter wind, ice beneath
my feet, wheels slipping downhill, the load
of children and old people wrapped in featherbeds,
couldn't understand what it meant
that the only "men" were under sixteen or over
sixty-five, that with each crossroad, the caravan
drifted apart, joined with others, that fate led
my grandmother and her children to refuge
in Czechoslovakia, four long weeks later.

III.

In May, the war over, we walked back home.

If only we had heard about the shifting border.

The occupiers called themselves our liberators.

No use talking about the beatings.

Too bad it took so long for the Poles to throw us out.

But the ones I blame are Hitler and his liars.

They stole my childhood and my future.

Silesia had been German for 700 years.

I'm one of the last to speak the dialect.

To make poppy seed dumplings.

To tell the story.

IV.

Even now, sometimes his sudden rage,
quaking voice, a tale I haven't heard:

early 1946, record cold, his father still missing,
his mother sending him for firewood to the forest—

place that had been his playground
where he'd picked berries, played hide and seek

or looked for boar tracks, broken twigs,
pretending to be the forester of his dreams—

stopped there by a young Polish guard yelling
in a simple German, *Mein Wald! Mein Wald!*—

My woods!—Father miming him for me,
shaking an invisible rifle with one hand,

pointing with the other at his proud, puffed chest,
finger jabbing his breastbone in time to the words.

Because I was washing my hands when she came through the door
and talked to my reflection: *I really liked the poem about your father.*

Because when I nodded *Thanks,* she pressed on, *I want you to know
I'm Jewish, that I've lived in both Israel and Prague, that I've*

never heard about any German suffering. Amazing, no? Because
I couldn't answer, remembering my stomach filled with stone,

shame in high school History, the film projector spinning endlessly
through *Night and Fog,* the black and white camps, bones,

speeches I didn't need subtitles to understand. Because I tasted
the grit again, the fluorescent lights harsh, honest

as her emotion: *And I want you to know it helps me somehow,
that German civilians suffered too, even children, like your dad.*

Because I knew what she meant. Because it still made me angry.
Because she had never seen my father's face, its map of worry,

his short stature from years of meager food. Because she called
my poem *important.* Because it can't be. Because she urged me

to write *more.* Because *more* overwhelms when my father recollects,
spreads to his father pressured to join the Brown Shirts in 1935,

quitting after the leader turned in his own brother for anti-Nazi talk,
a neighbor never seen again. Because my grandfather couldn't
    escape

his birth year of 1896, a second drafting into another world war,
capture in winter Russia where he lay sick and starving,

three men to each straw mattress. Because there's no comparing
the Russian camp to Auschwitz. Because my father once walked

through a train station, past a boxcar of whispering pleas: *Wasser,*
   Wasser.
Because he couldn't figure out why no one else heard, why no
   grown-ups

fetched water. Because on his way home, he forgot all about it.
Because I will never meet her father, grandfather, know their tales,

the ones she said *are always about the Holocaust, persecution—*
what the old people talk of, even at weddings, funerals.

Because it would have sounded dumb to tell her my father wept
at the movie *Fiddler on the Roof,* the slow procession out of the
   village,

a way of life, to explain how, in 1946, the towns and streets
were renamed behind him, cemeteries razed. Because, in the glare

of the mirror, my head even with hers, she offered, *Maybe it will be*
our generation who gets past the pain. Because she was younger

than me. Because I was tired. Because tonight, in a kink of fluke
or fate, I watch my son play *Tevye* on his high school stage,

in *kippah* and prayer shawl, singing of tradition, heartache,
glasses raised *To Life!*, my father at my side, his foot tapping along

in time. I wish I had reached out my hand, asked her name, looked
her in the eye before I left that restroom, returning to the crowd.

My father tells us a joke from wartime Germany:
Three boys are camping near a lake when a rowboat
carrying Goering, Goebbels, and Hitler starts to sink.
Each boy swims out, saves one man. On shore,
Goering asks his rescuer what he would like
as reward. "To become a pilot in your Air Force, Sir."
Then Goebbels asks the second boy, who replies,
"To become a director, make films of our Reich."
Finally, Hitler turns to the third boy. "I would like
a state funeral, please. When my father finds out
I saved your life, he's going to kill me."

The next week my son hears the same joke—
the characters changed to Rumsfeld, Cheney, Bush—
and when I mention this to an older friend,
he too recalls the punch line, the saved life

of Harry Truman. And it was just a few blocks from
Truman's house where my husband was made to play
a version of dodgeball—*Vietnam Bombardment,*
to fall down as soon as he was hit, the gym floor

littered with eighth-grade casualties. In Government
class, my son debates the push to war with teens
who believe *God is on our side.* I remember faith
put into lyrics—*The times they are a-changin'* . . .

Somewhere a boy is posing with an AK-47
for his martyr photo, while my sons, in the living
room, play a game of *Risk,* roll the dice,
advance little plastic soldiers. At ten, my father

hiked with schoolmates singing a Nazi anthem:
Our fallen comrades march among us in spirit.
Now he tells of a spirited neighbor he knew,
how her eighty-five years coincided

with four German wars, how she carefully
closed her windows and lowered her voice,
asking him to tell his joke, how she laughed
no matter how many times she heard it.

In the Village without a Typewriter

for my paternal grandmother,
Elfriede Dindas Misch (1903-1990)

I try to imagine the moment, in that farming village,
eastern Germany of 1944, when my grandmother

and her neighbor hatched their poem,
the rhymes my father remembers, translates:

> *A Schwabian was once called forth*
> *to reopen a cigar factory far to the north.*

I picture the two women in their babushkas,
heavy layered skirts, a cold wind in the yard,

my grandmother adding wood to the fire,
stirring the boiling cauldron of laundry,

watching, in the distance, the plump *Zigarrenmeister*
(title snickered behind his back)

yet again walk across fields rather than roads,
as if he could hide four years of visits

to the young war widow the way
his shy wife, in her wheelchair, hid at home.

> *But the bald little man, such a genius,*
> *took a pretty employee as his mistress.*

I wonder—lines written at my grandmother's
kitchen table, the children playing nearby—

if the ink turned shaky at the snare of his name,
Herr Reichert, his singsong dialect, his Nazi zeal,

Did you hear the latest speech he gave,
the Party's eager, steadfast knave?

and at the sudden grasp of a way to share their verse,
how no one would consider the teenaged secretary

who pedaled to work in the city, whom they trusted
to type several copies. Did either woman tremble

in the dark of midnight, at the noise of the hammer
as they nailed the poem to farmyard gates,

including the mayor's? Or were they thinking
he'd laugh too, resenting Reichert for carrying out

Goebbels's decree that any male, 16 to 60, not already
in uniform, enlist in the *Volkssturm,* attend all meetings.

Though when it comes to Volkssturm marching,
he sends a substitute to do his prancing.

The women heard scraps of government news
from those who owned a radio, but couldn't guess

at the depth of the danger, that Reichert would
announce: The author will be caught, taken away.

Permission for the only village gun makes him proud—
his head held high, ours bowed.

What they had been sure of was the act
they had witnessed with others that winter—

Reichert shooting a runaway Russian in a barn,
killing the starving soldier as he offered

a smile, shrugged shoulders, open hands,
bit of livestock potato in one, pocketknife in the other.

What I Wished For at Fourteen

my father in Silesia, August of 1945

I wished for food, something beyond
last year's potatoes—our only sustenance,
their pale skins, long eyes,
blind feelers digging through straw,
digging at air. I wished for bread.
I wished for salt.

I remembered how I used to wish
for adventure, but when Felix, the old poacher
in the village, offered for the first time
to take me hunting, I only wished for a deer
dumb enough to show itself in the clearing.
I wanted the smell and taste
and grease of meat.

I wished the Russians and the Poles
had never come. I wished they would leave.
Wasn't the war over? When were they going
to pack up their wagons, the gaunt horses
and cows they had brought, their police?

I wished to be fearless as Felix,
risking his life to hide a '98 Mauser rifle,
and as clever—rifle and ammunition tied
in an inner tube he pulled from a culvert pipe
near the forest, quickly unwrapping them
with his good hand, the other one
missing since the last war.

I wanted our whole house back,
not just the upstairs bedroom,
wanted it full again with furniture and pillows
and the pictures on the walls, the way everything

had looked before January 20th,
before we fled the Russian troops
only to return to Polish soldiers under our roof.

I wanted to stay awake all that night
in the deer blind, but Felix woke me
at the first hint of dawn, just before he fired.
I didn't know how loud it would be. I wished
my heart would stop pounding in my throat.

I wanted never to jump at another order
heaved at me, my mother, my brother and sisters
in a muddy, mangled German.
I wished not to be shoved.
I had stopped wishing for God
or for someone who cared about us.
I wanted to know if my father was alive.

As we followed the trail of blood,
I wanted to be first to find the deer.
And I still wanted it after the red stains ended
in the woods, Felix giving up, saying it was time for bed.
When we parted, I wanted the dog—*my* dog,
a stray that had shown up two days before,
who eagerly set off with me
along a different edge of the forest
on a narrow footpath I hadn't walked since fall.

I wished I could stop thinking about my uncle,
silent, his large fists trembling behind his back,
the two militia officers in a late-night visit
holding my cousin's arms, positioning his fingers
in the space between hinges,
and with their tall, black boots,
slowly closing the wooden door, bit by bit.

When the dog suddenly stopped, fur raised,
I already wanted to run back for Felix,

but then I saw, instead of a deer under the tree,
a man, one of the men who had stayed behind
in the winter to defend our village.

I did and didn't want to look at him,
his clothes—shoes pointed skyward,
corduroy pants, heavy jacket,
gray gloves strained at the tips,
fingernails or bones pushing against the wool—
and his head, a naked skull,
empty sockets staring right through me.

I shut my eyes and wished to erase him,
to erase the year, the last air-raid sirens in the city
when I knew I had to get on my bike,
pedal with planes overhead, school ending
for good, and Mother, hugging me tight,
opening the last jars of goose meat and fruit
she had been saving for my confirmation,
the party that had been planned for spring.

I wanted to erase the whole escape—our frantic slog
through snow, the strangers' wagons,
the crowded train that took us to Czechoslovakia,
to the hillside house where we stayed,
the windows and my insides rattling
when Dresden was bombed across the border.

I wished to forget the long, slow walk back in May,
how I pulled the handcart, my little sister and brother,
for weeks over mountains, along the Elbe, into cities
where we begged, Russian soldiers sometimes
throwing us a few slices of bread, the temperature
grown hot, street tar oozing between my toes,
green meadows dotted with birch-branch crosses,
helmets perched on top, and the villages
of burned-out houses or empty ones
where we searched for food and sleep.

When I opened my eyes, the body still there,
I wanted an explanation. I couldn't believe
the sun was warm on my face.
I couldn't believe the sky was blue
and full of birdsong.
I didn't want to find the deer.
I just wanted to go home.

My Father Talks of 1946

*Expulsion is the method which, in so far as we
have been able to see, will be the most satisfactory
and lasting. There will be no mixture of popula-
tions to cause endless trouble . . .*

WINSTON CHURCHILL, 1944, after Stalin
negotiated the expulsion of 15 million Germans
from their ancestral homelands in East and West
Prussia, Silesia, Pomerania, and the Sudetenland

The Poles loaded us into the same cattle cars
the Nazis had sent the other way.
They searched our sacks to make sure
there was nothing left worth stealing.
It was August 5th. A bit of bread
for what became a three-day ride.

Flüchtling—the word for refugee—
means one who flees, as if we had a choice,
or as if, after fifteen months of occupation,
soldiers taking over our house,
we weren't relieved to go.

Two million German civilians died
in the expulsion. Starvation, exposure,
torture, murder. You never hear of it.
Churchill kept his mouth shut.
And how could Germans talk about atrocity?

I was fifteen, suddenly a *Flüchtling*
in my own country, in a town where no one
understood our dialect, knew my surname.

Imagine it, if Texas were given to Mexico,
if the government delivered an El Paso mother
and four children to your door, ordered you
to give them a bedroom, share your empty pantry.

All I thought about was food.

Mother sent my sister and me out walking to the farms.
If they won't give you any potatoes, ask for only two.

The farmwomen scowled: *What will you do*
with only two? Oh here, take them!
When we had too many, we hid them in a ditch,
carried a few to show that others had given.

My aunt, who ended up in East Germany
with the other half of our village, sent me
my cousin's winter jacket. He had fallen
in Russia just before the war ended.

I had no shoes. Three times a week
Mother made me walk the hour
to the ration office. *Don't put anything*
on your feet or they'll never give you shoes.

Believe me, by November, it was cold.
I looked for grass to walk on
and dreaded the tile floor of the office,
the way adults tried to cut in front of me
because I wanted to stand on the doorway mat.

Don't think people didn't look out for themselves.

One day, the woman behind the window
whispered, *It's here,* snuck me out the back door
as she handed me the little certificate.

In the store, I picked out work shoes.
After years of *Learn! Learn!*
my parents no longer talked of school.

Bricklaying seemed like a good idea
in a land of rubble.

During Plans for War, Crows—

This flock, explicit ink
in a landscape of snow,

as if there were no buried layers,
grass and root, rock and bone,

immensity of time before *time,*
bird as *dinosaur,* evolution

leading to a scavenging strut,
head out of step, one shrill call,

the monotonous quest
to soar, sound of clapping

wings, conquered heights.
Consider the impact

from a gust of wind,
softness of a feather,

role of each fine strand
knit close as facts.

And if we love to hold
a feather, its subtle weight,

to run our fingers along the fringe,
feel the give and flow,

what tempts us to pull
the other way, unhinge the design,

snap open gaps, stark as winter,
the empty space filled with gray?

Poem in February

This is a poem for the librarian killed in Sarajevo
by shellburst as she tried to save rare books from flames,
for the gray-ash pages falling over the city, a man

catching one, feeling its heat before the words melted to dust,
for the apartment dwellers under siege, burning their books
to survive the winter—*two books to cook one pot of soup.*

This is a poem for my father, 14 in '45 Germany, lying on a roof,
searching clouds for the lost smells of bakery, butcher shop,
and for the same boy, seeing his uncle beaten and thrashed

by Russian police, hiding himself in a haystack with *The Last
of the Mohicans,* the first time he knew reading was escape.
This is a poem for my sister's cleaning lady, who sends money back

to the Ukraine for her 5-year-old son left behind two years ago,
and for my sister, who's stopped reading to her own young son
on Thursdays so that the Ukrainian woman won't watch and cry.

This is a poem for an old woman sitting on the subway,
pretending to read a newspaper, folding it over her knees, the run
in her hose trailing to shoes wrapped with duct tape,

and for the homeless man guarding his spot, his table
on the sidewalk, selling magazines and books
found in the trash—*Gourmet, Vogue, The Big Picture.*

A welder in Moldova hasn't been paid in 3 years.
He has 1 wife, 1 child, and 2 kidneys.
Calculate the cost for his travel to Turkey,
the sale of 1 kidney for 30 years' wages.

The Japanese use 12 distinct sets
of words for numbers, based on the shape
of what's being counted. Determine if sacrifice
is a cylinder, a surface, or a bowl.

Compute the likelihood the British soccer player
who bought the kidney fears death
more than the Moldovan does.

Stalin said, *A single death is a tragedy, a million deaths
a statistic.* Prove his theory using AIDS victims.
Solve for grief in Africa.

Edvard Munch painted different versions of *The Scream.*
Plot the size of the howls against
the intensity of the blood-red sky.

In 1202, Fibonacci discovered a mathematical sequence,
the pattern obeyed by sunflower petals, pinecone whorls.
Analyze technology, minimalist zeroes and ones,
for the same kind of beauty.

Your dishwasher breaks on Monday.
At Appliance World, the salesman tells you 3 times
he'll give you 2 free boxes of detergent if you buy today.
If you don't, what is the probability
his family will eat macaroni & cheese all week?

What is the extravagance-to-guilt ratio when a) a multimillionaire
buys a baby-sized Gucci leather biker's jacket for $1500?
b) you buy a double caffe latte for $3?

Assume Hawking is right—humans, Earth's kudzu vine,
won't survive the next millennium unless they colonize space.
Write an equation to show who goes, who stays.

II.

[The soldier] is shining his boots. He sits on the edge of his bunk . . .
And, bending over himself, he is his own nest . . .
His boots are bright already, yet still he rubs
And rubs till, brighter still, they are his mirror . . .

DAVID FERRY

Waiting

There is no terror in the bang,
only in the anticipation of it.
ALFRED HITCHCOCK

I turn on the radio and listen to Janet Leigh
admit in these forty years since *Psycho*
she has only bathed, never showered—

life changed by pretending,
the Bates Motel set, bathroom jammed
with cameras and crew, knife-thrusts

lunging at shadow. But who can
forget her screams? Long. Real
as the way she now says *vulnerable*—

each syllable more frightening,
the way she pauses before
naked and *slippery-wet.*

She says, *In a shower you can't hear*
beyond the water, can't see beyond
the curtain, the mind a rush

of thoughts, a drape of logic,
flimsy attempts at blocking out fear,
the unknown that part of us

is waiting for. And isn't every thriller
a rewrap of Schadenfreude—glee
in someone else's panic, in our dull days?

I imagine poor Janet in the tub,
nervous even there, her ready hand
pressed against cold tiles, silence

broken by the slowly dripping faucet,
one glassy droplet, growing heavy,
my distorted face reflected back.

Self-Portraits, Three-Way Mirror

the engineer remembers the rumble:

indoor engines, full-throttle roar,

torque, speed, temperature,

everything cause and effect,

fear of her own analysis—

oil leak, broken crankshaft,

which came first?, real life

problems unlike the kind in books,

the comfort of balanced equations,

variables and constants—

each bearing their own small history,

strange names, a value beyond

inquiry, the necessary trust

of assumption to gain a greater

answer, the calculated quest for

a certain and safe design

the poet recalling childhood—

a secret space between

two pines, thrill of hiding,

the tunnel, pungent green

branches scratching her skin,

a longing for something more than

needles, their posture of protection,

the stories she told herself,

complicated daydreams, recurring

themes, she the hero—ponders doubts,

the bright fur of *caterpillar,*

surprise in the pull-push crawl

or is it creep? of her thoughts,

skip of her pen veering away from

time, place, the notebook lines

she is bound to ignore

girls weren't allowed to wear pants
to school. The teenager next door, three vast
years older than me, wouldn't explain
who she meant when she said her *friend*
was visiting again. Her mother,
Charlotte, in curlers on her porch,
bottle tucked under the chair, told me,
Honey, don't start shaving your legs
or the blonde hairs will turn black, ugly.
I wanted to be Samantha on *Bewitched*,
have secret powers, an adoring husband,
and that hairdo, the flip of a wave
instead of two drooping braids
Mom wove each morning,
her hands pulling too tight.
She hated dusting, gave me the job,
including the stairs that led to our renter,
Miss Jean, her flat a world in pinks
smelling of perfume, cigarettes, candy.
I wondered why she wasn't married,
how a lady as lovely as the one framed
on her dressing table became an *old maid*.
When Tony, boy from down the street,
gave me a turtle as a gift, retrieved my cap
from laughing bullies, and stood at my door,
singing *Close to You*, I blushed
for a week from the teasing. I quit
taking accordion lessons without telling
anyone the old Italian teacher
kissed me on the lips. In my book
of fairy tales, the girl who cheerfully
did all the work was showered
with gold, the lazy sister covered with tar,
the patient princess rescued. I dreamed

of being brave as a prince or an astronaut
or the missing soldier whose name I wore
on a bracelet, silver glinting while I tried
to climb the giant rope in Gym,
but only hung there, stuck, *like a girl,*
fibers scratching through my tights.

So now it's come to this—Sharon Olds
in black suit and pearls, reading
to me and a full auditorium
about the topography of her
and her husband's bodies together
in bed while I pant alone
in my basement in an old T-shirt
and shorts, stepping up one
plastic stair only to step right
back down before climbing up again,
getting nowhere, like the pet mouse
Olds wrote of, its burial
after all that wheel-turning.
My whirring mind sweats as I listen
and wonder if Sharon, in her tallness,
ever exercises or feels she should,
and what she would think of me,
the sounds of my breath and footfalls
mingling with her words.
Sharon, I've watched your tape
at least a dozen times, your cadence,
though not the beat of rock, urging
me to move, to push heavy weights
over my head and out from my heart,
to consider all the people who
would choose any music over poetry,
who have never heard of you
or Galway Kinnell and the taste
of his icy, black blackberries,
who live life without struggling
to write about it, until I don't know
who's the wiser—them or me
forming a poem as I crunch through sit-ups,
listening now to Czeslaw Milosz

whose muscles never tired of the strain—
"Reality, what can we do with it?"

In the Morning Paper

Mohammed Sesay, age 29
Freetown, Sierra Leone, January 1999

His eyes question the camera—eyes that five days ago
watched two friends turn rebel, storm the house,

shoot eight in his family. He begged them, *Kill me now.*
They pressed one arm, then the other, atop a tree stump.

Already he's relived the moments countless times: Sun-glare
on the machete. A butcher-quick whir. The blade thudding

into wood. And pain—a thousand hot needles—before the dark
cloud of sleep. He woke in the hospital to the smell of blood.

He sits in boxer shorts on a cot, ribcage showing, shoulders
slumped. Two slings—white cloth, torn thin—hang round

his neck, criss-cross his chest to cradle empty fists
of gauze. He misses his mother most, wonders how long

his brother will feed him, bathe him, dress him.
Last night as he slept, a mosquito bit his thigh.

His fingers reached and scratched, waking him to remember
he would never pick a berry, lift a shovel, caress a lover.

He will not see this photograph, his own steady gaze
or mine, as I read, drink coffee, turn the page.

Girl in the Photograph

This Indian child earns about 86 cents
for every 1,000 bricks she carries.
THE NEW YORK TIMES

On your head, a thick wooden disk,

flat square of stone, and seven bricks

in layers of two, the odd one towering

on one side. You hold your small

shoulders straight, hands gripping

the bottom bricks, crust chafing

your fingertips. Eyelids almost closed,

you watch the ground. How many

steps for a loaf of bread? How

many hours until your arms go numb?

I want to feed you soup and cake,

bathe you, tuck you into bed,

rubbing your back until you sleep,

wishing you dreams of flight, your body

weightless above dirt and stones.

To My Son, in His Garden

for Rob, July 2003

Crouched in the tangle of vines,
you search for marble-sized hints
of cantaloupe—*baby melons.*
Sixteen years ago, you were born
to the spring's first thunder.
This is a season of firsts:
girlfriend, car, paychecks,
a war you read about each morning
over breakfast, and the garden,
your money going for peat and seeds,
plants and a coil of fence tall enough
to keep out deer. Watching you
surrounded by the metal mesh,
I remember the soft weave
of net in that old, blue playpen
keeping you safe. But heavy-duty
fencing is no barrier to carrot fungus,
cold spells, windstorm—stalks of corn
blown into a heap of matchsticks.
Your girlfriend ill, too, tethered
to a heart monitor.
                  All winter
you studied catalogs, their gleaming
bounty guaranteed under normal
growing conditions. How anxious
you were for the break from alarm clock
and textbooks, time to dig
in the dirt, to cultivate
summer days easy as the ones
when you caught toads and bugs,
made little nests of grass
in shoebox homes, gave the creatures
pep talks when letting them go free.

Heading out to the garden,
you announce a couple times a day,
to weed or water, visit the hope
of harvest. Do you remember
the cherry tomatoes I once grew,
your eyes level with the fruit,
bright red globes you plucked,
pushed into your mouth faster
than you could eat? Now we wait
for the taste of *Supersteak,*
Bigger Boy, Heirloom, the measured
rows disappearing, tendrils everywhere
demanding taller stakes. You tighten
your chest, slide in sideways, look to see
where to place one foot, then the other.

I could start with the bullet, the first thing
I think of, the easy way she talked of it
twenty years ago. Or I could mention the headlines
in today's paper, a Detroit child shot dead,
a little girl on her porch, the street name
almost familiar. Perhaps I should say
I live forty miles from the city,
that I drive downtown maybe twice a year,
that I haven't been back to the neighborhood
I grew up in since 1974 when my parents
moved us to the suburbs, far from where
she and I turned cartwheels on car-sized
front yards, jumped, to avoid bad luck,
over cracks in the sidewalk. Is it too sentimental
to include me, at her front door, calling *Su-san,*
the smell of her *Nonna*'s tomato sauce and apron,
the scratch of the braided rug in her room,
sun dappling in through eyelet curtains
as we played with baby dolls and Barbie,
rehearsing the future? If I admit I only imagine
the curtains, does it make our time together
less authentic, less tender? Better, I suppose,
a pulled-up shade, sun intense
as the letters we wrote when I moved,
teenage secrets penned every day, sealed
with wax, an initial or a heart. Does it matter
how long it took for letters to taper
to cards to unsent wedding invitations?
Or that it was she who eventually looked me
up, drove the hour to visit, brought pictures
of her children? What stays from that afternoon
are her gold ball earrings, two tiny worlds,
and her talk of life in the city: the rented flat across
from Denby High, gang fights in the parking lot,

how one morning she found a bullet in the crib,
a hole in the screen of the open window,
her baby asleep at the other end of the mattress.
What good to picture her holding the bullet,
cold metal rolling in her palm as she watched
her baby breathe? To realize it's my infant son
I see lying there in shadows of *chance* and *fate*,
my mind chasing after reason, as if finding a cause
could make up for the ending: I waved from my porch
as she drove away, knew I wouldn't phone
as promised, our friendship frozen
like a cartwheel mid-turn, my lawn too vast,
too green, no sidewalks heaved up by roots.

"Another Good Kid Shot Dead in Detroit"

DECEMBER HEADLINE

We tally, chalk the sum—
the 28th child this year.
Honor student, football player, poet, dancer—
his march no longer present tense.

The 28th child this year,
a job at Skateland, an easy smile,
his march, no longer present tense,
the walk home, a crunch through snow.

A job at Skateland, an easy smile,
the weight of his mother's dreams
as he walked home, crunched through snow.
Will his sister become the doctor now?

The weight of his mother's dreams,
the hip brand of cap and jacket.
Will his sister become the doctor now?
She says, *I will do it for Mario.*

The hip brand of cap and jacket,
a poem folded inside a pocket.
She says, *I will do it for Mario.*
The bullet was meant for someone else.

Folded inside a pocket, a poem
about songs in city noises, in his heart.
The bullet, meant for someone else—
he ran until he collapsed.

Hearing songs in city noises, in his heart,
a boy imagines himself a man.
He ran until he collapsed,
took his last breaths alone.

How to imagine him as a man—
honor student, football player, poet, dancer,
the song of his last breaths, alone?
We tally, chalk the sum.

In Code

*It was the complex software created at Michigan's
Gene Codes Corporation that made most of the
1,571 successful World Trade Center victim iden-
tifications possible . . . This week the Gene Codes
staff is working on Version 137 of the software
called Mass-Fatality Identification System,
M-FISys, pronounced emphasis.*

DETROIT FREE PRESS, SEPTEMBER 9, 2004

If   the latest shipment,
                                      tiny vials cradling
                                      flecks of charred bone,
                                      pinches of dust
=True
Then   the work of processing
                                      presses on,
                                      even into dreams
Execute
Data File Path   faces of parents, siblings, children
                                      silently opening their mouths to offer
                                      a swab of their cells,
                                      the tangible scrape
                                      of something carried within
Go To
Private Menu   your four-year-old son
                                      building towers of LEGO,
                                      knocking them over
                                      with his Fisher-Price plane
Subroutine
Prompt   the anniversary, interviews
                                      about company sacrifice—
                                      lost profits, eighty-hour weeks,
                                      colleagues burnt out, moving on
Inner Join
System

Show   a plastic model of the double helix,
Try   an example you recite by heart:
                  AGTGGGCTACGTGGA . . .
Repeat   *the process of identifying remains*
                  will be magnitudes faster next time
Timer Enabled
Catch As Exception   the search for comfort,
Store   *Good-bye . . . I love you . . .*
Do While
Static Counter   sequence matching,
                  matching sequence,
Open Dialog   what to emphasize beyond
Function>   our nature, our language,
Message As String   spiral rungs, incessant twists,
                  weave, unraveling
Ignore
Namespace   letters of thanks,
                  personal effects
Read Only
Object Stream   hope packaged in manila envelopes,
Description Hold in a lipstick or razor, toothbrush or
                  pillowcase a spouse folded
                  and smelled for the last time
                  or maybe the first
End If

III.

There is courtship, and there is hunger. I suppose
there are grips from which even angels cannot fly.
Even imagined ones . . .
MARY SZYBIST

Wren's Nest in a Saguaro

Not art but necessity
    creates a home
        amid giant thorns,

the layered twigs,
    dried roots,
        bits of tumbleweed

a palette of Arizona browns
    in the slender space
        between stem

and candelabra arm.
    Imagine flying in
        and out of spikes,

feathers grazing barbs
    until they're woven
        over, transformed

into brace, a partnership,
    choreography of plant
        and animal—

cactus offering its hollow,
    bird filling it—
        the need to build

shelter for young
    as vital as the need
        to free pollen

by luring beak and wing,
    leaving us
        the need to witness,

to name the dance
    efficient, elegant,
        the wren's flight *brave.*

My father ordered into a chair,
my mother and I escorted to the other end
   of the hall—a tiny office, door closed,

I sat on her lap and tried not to look
at the stiff, brown uniform hovering over us,
   the guard's fingers opening our suitcase,

touching all the gifts my grandmother had given us
that day: pajamas, picture book, a wooden puzzle.
   In formal German, thick with politeness,

he began, *Sie wissen doch . . . You know, of course . . .*
No printed materials! No toys or slippers!
   No subsidized goods allowed out of the country!

And he knew, of course, from my mother's
American passport (Place of birth: Germany),
   from our visit to relatives, that my mother

must have escaped sometime before the wall.
Ten years earlier, at seventeen, she'd told officials
   she was again going to visit her grandparents

in the west, instead took a plane to the man
she would marry, man she had met only once, known
   through his letters. Her mother had been relieved—

one less child to worry about, the youngest
who, as a toddler, was left home alone in a playpen,
   who, as a teenager, still sucked her thumb.

The guard didn't know or care that my grandmother
now worked as a *Toilettenfrau* in the restroom of a hotel,
   handing out toilet paper, cleaning up after women

and men who came to eat in the restaurant, dance
in the ballroom. Sometimes she slept in a chair
    between the two rows of stalls so as not to miss

any late night or early morning tips, saving
the pennies and wages to buy gifts for her children
    and grandchildren more often than she bought food.

I'd seen my mother open the packages at home
when they came in the mail, shake her head
    at the trinkets, at the martyred family photographs—

the track of my grandmother's scissors
where she had cut herself out of the pictures.
    And I had watched my mother that afternoon

give my grandmother a necklace—or try to,
my grandmother holding my mother's wrists,
    not letting the gold clasp be brought around her neck,

the struggle lasting until they were both red
in the face, out of breath, my mother giving up,
    stuffing the crumpled necklace into her pocket.

The guard, relentless, demanded my grandmother's
name, address *for further investigation.* My mother refused,
    began to cry, and I realized she too, was scared

but when my own tears followed, she fought back,
stood and faced the guard, spoke in his deliberate
    manner: *Sir, I know just what to do. I'll turn around,*

walk this suitcase back one block and dump
the contents into the nearest trash can. Then you can
    let us proceed, all the problems discarded.

The guard's eyes narrowed to the insult—
East German products unwanted, not good enough
    for an American—though he relaxed his voice:

Now, now, we mustn't have that either. My mother
seized the chance, insisted. When the guard told us
to repack the bag, to go, I ran ahead into my father's arms

while my mother made her way behind me, up
the narrow hall, struggling with the suitcase—its weight,
every other step, hitting hard against her leg.

What I'm sure of is
   playing in the front yard,
      the vastness of the days,

twirling myself, arms outstretched
   in a game called *helicopter*
      which wasn't about flight

but power. I must have noticed
   the other kids called home
      for lunch, their curtains

and windows open, their mothers
   dressed; mine sitting
      in her nightgown, in the dark.

On tiptoe, I turned my fastest,
   releasing houses and maples
      from their stoic poses,

blurring the neighborhood
   into a wild kaleidoscope
      I commanded.

Best was losing to dizziness,
   my body falling
      to the smell of grass,

of earth—a giant wave
   tilting me in every direction,
      colors dissolving in the sky.

Too soon, rooftops floated
    back among branches, the world
      slowing to standstill,

the way I'd slow—told only
    Mom was *sick*—then spin
      again, a nauseous comfort.

two parents plus two daughters, even on Christmas Eve
when we read aloud greetings from relatives across
the ocean, Dad making a ritual out of slicing the marzipan
Schwein to bring us luck, the taste launching

his talk about wartime hunger, childhood trauma,
Mom joking about hers. We laughed over their wedding,
how they had borrowed ten dollars to take to the courthouse,
how the Justice had insisted Mom—seventeen, not knowing

any English—repeat the nonsense syllables
the way my sister and I sang along to German
folksongs in the car, babbling some of the lyrics
we'd realize later we had wrong. And we taught them

the things we learned about in school: white bread
with peanut butter and jelly, square dancing,
homecoming, the difference between *sip* and *zip*,
lettuce and *letters*—like the ones I longed to read,

the tied-with-string bundle high in their closet,
see-through envelopes I just knew smelled of love,
the house full of aromas—*Kaffee* and homemade *Suppe*
Mom poured into Dad's thermoses every morning,

mud and fresh cement on his work boots, Epsom-
salted water she carried to the family room for him
to soak his feet before she trimmed his nails.
And the foul silences that followed their arguments.

I imagine Dad burned the letters when I was thirty,
when he warned me *Die Geschichte ist vorbei,*
the story finished, *and the ending can't be happy*—
word, even now, a dozen years after divorce, he never

uses to describe himself. *Happy is an American idea.*
He seeks to be *content.* At Christmas, Mom sends me
Lebkuchen—cake for living?—chocolate coated
gingerbread shaped into hearts—nothing like the practical

muscle, its distinct chambers, beat of survival no longer
child's play, those houses I constructed from paper,
cutting windows to open like an Advent calendar,
four smiling faces drawn in crayon underneath.

At Sway

Before air conditioning, the city sidewalks
alive with hopscotch, two-square,

monkey in the middle, with grown-ups
hurrying to the store or the bus stop,

I used to sway on daisied vinyl cushions,
an old metal glider that had somehow—

like our renter—come with the house,
glider I loved as much as the front porch,

a covered, roosted room open
to leaves and dragonflies and breeze,

to the sounds of neighbors, of parents,
fights and, sometimes, laughter,

sometimes rain—magical to stay dry,
suddenly cool with storm all around,

rumbles and crashes, the wet smell
of the world, water flooding gutters

and curbs, plunging everywhere at once,
like my heart, at all it longed to know—

the questions themselves, balls thrown
just above my head, beyond my reach . . .

Today, in the frost of middle age,
I drive back and forth—the first time

in thirty years—on the street of my youth,
trying hard to recognize the few houses

that haven't been demolished, the treeless
lots, and wondering what I might be

looking for in the spot—grown so small—
where the porch must have stood,

where the sweet creak of the glider
has turned to *then, now, then, now.*

This Winter

A mouse nest in the piano.
My mother depressed again.

What to do but stick my hand
inside, tear at the thicket

of cocoon, ask her, long-
distance, if she's showered, eaten?

I shudder at the gray, gnawed felt,
splinters of wood, pink insulation,

and tell her about the snow,
banked so high this year.

I keep her on the line,
picture the mouse squeezing

through the gap around a pedal,
scampering for dark. She asks, *Why*

now? after a decade of lithium,
trading spirit for a little peace.

The traps—damn it!—empty for days,
the pantry cluttered. I need to think

each time I crack open the door,
a box of cereal, bag of pretzels,

listen to her voice, thin and slow
as ice melt, the muffled tone

of a sudden stuck key.

Middle School Band Concert

Their uniforms—starched white shirts,
   black bow ties, cummerbunds—
      shine on a stage with chairs and stands

crammed close, young bodies merged
   into one great whole, while the tall girl,
      standing in back, waits, waits

to deliver a crash of her cymbals,
   their timbre meant to rouse
      like the march being played,

the baton insisting along with the push
   and pull of the teacher's palm,
      melody secondary to precision,

proof of lessons learned, the gleaming
   slides of the trombones synchronized,
      unlike the drums that pound within,

or the rumble of applause as parents, unable
   to hear their child's isolated notes, rise,
      eager to say *Good job!* or *Next time,*

sit up straighter!, knowing tomorrow,
   when the students watch their performance
      on video, the teacher will grade

their rhythm, their emotion, reminding
   them about medals they can pin above
      their hearts if everyone's music

starts and stops at exactly the same time.
   And now, as they exit, the backs
      of their heads are dark and dreadful

like the whispers resuming in the lobby
about the 7th-grader who hanged himself
at home over the weekend.

For My Son, at Twelve

Alone, out back, you play football,
                 kick, then chase wild bounces,
the tough-skinned ball.
                 You throw it high, run and lunge,
commit your body to the catch,
                 no matter the landing.
What is it about falling you love?
                 When you were two, I scolded *No*
crashing! And yesterday, at ping-pong—
                 the concrete floor!—I threatened to quit
if you didn't stop diving. You didn't
                 stop. And I kept right on aiming
for the corners, your amazing saves.
                 I watch from the window as you rush
toward a ghost-load of opponents,
                 outmaneuver them with swerve and spin,
dreams of valor—the announcer shouting
                 Touchdown! past the linden tree,
autumn leaves cheering in the wind.
                 The clock is running, Jamie,
and I still can't grasp the rules,
                 the shifting line of scrimmage
between us, turns at offense and defense,
                 your yardage, my fumbles.

Night Poem

Insomnia is an endless
   field of harvest
      stubble. A whirling

eddy of leaves,
   rustle of spirits
      skipping on stone.

Will I ever stop replaying
   the hurtful words
      I spoke this morning

or the radio's Motown—
   Nowhere to run,
      nowhere to hide . . . ?

Does wind, like love,
   change its howl
      with the seasons,

with night? Or does it
   only sound colder
      because I want it to?

What I really want
   is a cup of my mother's
      cure-all chamomile tea.

How is it I've grown
   to crave tastes
      I hated in childhood?

I see the home movie
    where I play at bricklaying,
        try to whistle like Dad

alongside him—how much
    time do I have left
        with my parents?

The language of night
    is creaks, breath,
        silence . . . We say

unable to sleep,
    as if letting go is skill
        instead of gift,

as if the mind can help
    its greedy quest
        for more

than the thin skin
    of eyelids or the rub
        of calloused feet.

To the Previous Owner

upon buying a used copy of
Mark Doty's Sweet Machine

Amusing, the words you underlined
afloat on penciled rafts,
your captain's voice hovering
behind my chair, pointing out voyage
highlights—the way Doty placed *stubborn*
between *sheer* and *nerve,* how he
defended his use of *luster and gleam*—
your scattered exclamation points
like confident masts, shouts of Land ho!

But here, on page seventy-two,
in the margin of the elegy's last stanza,
disappointment crests your scrawl:
The emotion is too earnest.
As if grief should be kept hidden—
a mystery like you—a faceless compass,
a map impossible to unroll.
As if poetry could be charted
away from particular rocks
and rivers, the rapids too much.

See, you've got me doing it, loading
that heavy cargo of *too.* Useless,
of course, to interrogate your markings,
their abrupt ending, midbook.
Still, I'm curious about the poems
I suspect you write, the trailing wake
of your images, how you measure
their sincerity, what you'd think of mine.

Perhaps you've tired of sailing
against the wind, some private gale

sending you below deck, Doty's book
abandoned. Or perhaps someone else
sold the book, an heir or friend who never
noticed your final scribble, a stubborn buoy
warning of the unsafe waters
of perception, your question mark
gleaming under the poem's last word—*true.*

IV.

Science has done absolutely nothing about noise. The worst design flaw in the human body is that you can't close your ears. The reason you can't close your ears is, if a lion was coming, you had to wake up. Today no lions are coming. Beeping trucks are coming.

FRAN LEBOWITZ

Don't worry, be happy.
Sometimes you feel like a nut, sometimes you don't.
Another day in paradise.
Peace with honor.

Sometimes you feel like a nut, sometimes you don't.
Whole lotta shakin' goin' on.
Peace with honor.
Take your family to Disney World.

Whole lotta shakin' goin' on.
When you say Budweiser, you've said it all.
Take your family to Disney World.
What's love got to do with it?

When you say Budweiser, you've said it all.
It's the economy, stupid.
What's love got to do with it?
Winning hearts and minds.

It's the economy, stupid.
Do you believe in magic?
Winning hearts and minds.
A thousand points of light.

Do you believe in magic?
Put a tiger in your tank.
A thousand points of light.
Welcome to Marlboro Country.

Put a tiger in your tank.
Let the sunshine in.
Welcome to Marlboro Country.
How do you spell relief?

Let the sunshine in.
Mission accomplished.
How do you spell relief?
Be all you can be.

Mission accomplished.
In the still of the night.
Be all you can be.
Let freedom ring.

In the still of the night.
Billions and billions served.
Let freedom ring.
Burning down the house.

Billions and billions served.
Who's crying now?
Burning down the house.
It keeps going and going and going . . .

Who's crying now?
Say it with flowers.
It keeps going and going and going . . .
You can't always get what you want.

Say it with flowers.
Limited collateral damage.
You can't always get what you want.
Dancing in the streets.

Limited collateral damage.
Still crazy after all these years.
Dancing in the streets.
My dog's bigger than your dog.

Still crazy after all these years.
Don't worry, be happy.
My dog's bigger than your dog.
Another day in paradise.

Imagining Her Letter

a 78-year-old writes from New Orleans

Dear Mr. President of the Stearns and Foster Company,
I thank you for making a mattress that floats.
For eight days, I sailed around my bedroom in nothing
but underclothes. My muumuu, like everything, got soaked
that first day at breakfast—I'd eaten two spoonfuls of cereal—
when the water started flowing in. Five minutes later
it was five feet deep. All my furniture, including the bed
and mattress in the guest room, sank. Without
my Stearns and Foster (the extra firm model I only bought
last April), I would have sat all those days and nights
clinging to my ladder. Instead, I climbed the rungs
to a queen-sized island. Each morning, I had
a handful of raisins, a bite of cheese, and one estimated
glass of water I sipped slowly from the jug. The rest
of the time I didn't let myself think about food, a trick
I remember trying when I was a girl and very poor.
But you see, at 17, I went north, worked for forty-two years
before moving back, filling a ten-room ranch—just me
and my stuff. I owned silk pajamas (never worn!),
two full-length mink coats, six TVs. I loved my TVs.
So I was surprised when I didn't miss them, not once.
I just kept on floating, thinking about all kinds of things,
especially colors. I watched the pink paint on my walls
change to rose with the setting sun, my legs gleam
in the dawn, the water shining black or gray-green
or black again. Even the hours seemed tinted—mostly orange,
like the wings of a moth that came to visit one afternoon.
The prettiest, palest shade of orange I've ever seen.
Oh sure, sometimes I talked to myself: "Well, Louann,
now you look at that ceiling, the dust and cobweb
you didn't sweep away." My ceiling looked different
up close. I'd never noticed a tiny mark shaped almost
like a star. "Twinkle, twinkle," I started singing, amazed

that my throat still knew how, that I could be older
than kind Miss Hawkins was, back when she taught me
that song. I wondered what happened to the other kids,
if Annie Jones and the slow boy, Tom, might somehow
be in the city yet, maybe floating on a mattress just like me.
I wasn't scared, Sir. Just thought you'd like to know.

Tuning

I try to tune out the *boom! boom! boom!*
  from the shooting range two miles from my house,
    and think of the people who live next door

to the targets, or in the din of London and Berlin
  where nightingales now sing fourteen decibels louder
    to be heard by mates, quintupling the pressure

in their lungs. I've never heard a nightingale,
  but I know *noise* came from *nausea,* and *bull's-*
    eye names the goal for some blurry desire.

Bullseye is a band in Norway playing *gung-ho rock and roll,*
  like the kid down the street whose car speakers rumble
    through his closed windows and mine,

drums pummeling our insides. If I told him I once hiked
  among redwoods, heard ghostly calls in the stillness,
    branches somewhere in the canopy sky

moaning as they swayed, would he say *Cool*
  or *Whatever,* the way my sons have mumbled it,
    intending that I shouldn't—or maybe should—hear,

all talk target practice, ricochet and sashay, headache
  and heartache, duck and cover. In a fable, Lion realizes
    too late his vulnerability, the tunnel of his ear,

tiny Mosquito zooming in. Out beyond Pluto, Voyager's
  golden disc offers mud pots, thunder, footsteps,
    a Brandenburg Concerto and *Johnny B. Goode.*

Was the very first song a hum or a shout, laughter
  or weeping? When my friend, at forty, praised
    her cochlear implants, she complained about work,

the ringing office phones—*How do people concentrate?*
    I consider her vacations—wind surfing, rock climbing,
        marathons—how different now that she hears

each splash and scrape, the *huh* of heavy exhalation.
    I wish I could adorn my ears the way warriors in India did,
        with metallic green beetle wings, an iridescent

clacking and tinkling at the Feast of Courage. Imagine
    if we could hear bread rising, dew forming, the budding
        of raspberries, the tear of a cocoon, a minnow's pulse,

our own cells growing, dying. When my husband
    kisses my ear, I love the swoosh, the quiver, his breath
        sand driven by wind, my whispered name.

I marvel at all the accomplishments
of my alternate selves: *Christine Rhein,*
Figure Skating Champion of Rockford, Illinois
and *Vice President, Board of Directors,*
State Bank of Mishicot, Wisconsin.
How comforting to know, in other parts
of the Midwest, I've not only learned
how to skate a perfect double axel
but also, finally, to balance
a checkbook, perhaps performing
both feats at the same time.
                            At the *Turkey Night*
Grand Prix in Las Vegas, *Chris Rhein*—
balding and in need of a shave—
is posed beside a midget race car,
a testosterone-red *Cavalier Connection.*
OK, so I came in 30th (out of 34)
but at least I used *an Ecotec engine*
running on methanol alcohol fuel.
                            In Germany,
I am *Doktor Rhein* with a paper on *Aortic Root*
Surgery: Comparison of valve-sparing
reimplantation versus composite grafting,
and also *Fitness Leader Rhein* explaining
her Frankfurt program via *Translate this page:*
Because the perseverance range various,
and who already puts the sports badge down
three times has, silver gets, before there is
gold medal starting from the fifth time.
                            The real me
offers an occasional motion at a meeting
of the *Brighton High School PTA,*
a contribution to the *Friends of the Library,*
some poem titles in journal archives,

and—oh yes, an *honorable mention*
for *Woodpecker,* its short lines,
a crazy Morse code . . .
                    everyone busy hammering,
busy nodding, as I am at the fitness instructor's
website banner: *The activities are so varied*
that actually for each person
somewhat among the facts
it should be that there is joy.

Again he startles me,
mid-stanza,
words left hanging,
rhythm lost
to his rapid-fire knocks,
a crazy Morse code.
I curse this bird
who doesn't know
house from tree.
Three times this morning
I've opened the window,
rattled the blinds,
shouted him away.
He doesn't understand
his one-note scolds
are not the bones
of poetry.
Not oriole,
all color and song.
He can't help
his shadow-gray feathers,
his diligent digging.
He's hungry.
Let him bore
into the wood,
hammer out
o after *o* after *o*
in straight little rows
as he hunts for food
he cannot see—
is the taste
always a surprise?

Artiste Maurice Bennett Explains His "Burning Desire"

a picture of the Mona Lisa on the side
of a building using 2,124 slices of toast

I know what you're thinking—
wasn't it bad enough?—her likeness
stamped on socks and shower curtains,
shaped into cookie jars, mustached
in milk or with matching goatee,
morphed into *Mona Lewinsky*
and pink Muppet *Mona Pigga*.
But this is different. This is Art, inspired,
yes, by an overtoasted piece of *Wonder,*
my knife scraping away charred crumbs,
revealing flesh tones underneath—
bread gone *chiaroscuro,* features
emerging from shadow, patterns of singe.
Though don't think it's easy, browning
thousands of squares to specific hues,
or burning them—black and blacker—
without setting off the smoke alarm,
and arranging all those right angles,
so unlike the contours of her shoulders,
her bosom, which alone measures 18 by 27
luscious slices—my happiest days
on the scaffold, engulfed, dwarfed
by her dough-beige cleavage.
Picture the tension, the crowd watching
as I assembled her giant eyes watching them
no matter where they stood. And then the vast
mystery of her smile, lips I longed to kiss
despite their yeast-formed craters.
It's true—I love her. I've even tasted
her, her crunch melting on my tongue,
her voice whispering in my dreams

where, there too, I protect her from mold
and birds, as I magically float about her,
my Lisa, my darling, my toast.

Friday night

and we're not perched at some neon-lit Manhattan bar,
not dancing in the ballroom of the San Francisco Ritz

but mixing martinis in our Michigan kitchen,
a pot of potatoes on the stove, our twenty-year-old

formica piled with newspapers, bills, sons' projects—
bean plants growing well beyond the experiment.

I think of all the variables affecting a marriage . . .
How lucky to sit at this counter, to watch you

lift the frosted glasses from the freezer, your hips
moving in rhythm as you bounce the deco shaker,

its jangle of gin and ice—and that drop of liqueur
you add, tinting the cocktails robin egg blue.

As If

after images from the book Powers of Ten

It begins
        as if love were at the core—
an overhead shot of a picnic,
sunlit man and woman napping
amidst grapes and cheese, baguette
and wine, a Hershey's bar shining
from the open basket, details
arranged for contrast,
               the next page
a leap into space, the picnic rendered
10^{25} meters away. I study the number:
10,000,000,000,000,000,000,000,000—
ten septillion, the vast blackness,
the occasional speck of a tiny white
galaxy, as if there's nothing
more
        than clotted dust to turn
through—three pages and three fewer
zeroes later—to reach the thumbprint
of the Milky Way, dense spiral,
a hundred billion stars scattering
into points, frame after frame
of sameness,
           as I race to *our* sun,
our solar system, the reassuring
mist of Earth, swirl of white on blue
filling the page, the familiar shape
of Lake Michigan, size of a raindrop,
or a tear?
        As if acquaintance casts
the gloss on scenes from satellite:
luminous cities, grid of streets, rail lines
trekking along downtown Chicago, dots

of cars on Lake Shore Drive, the lawn
at Soldier Field,
                    and, yes, the picnickers,
still dreaming there together
until, at one meter, there's just enough
perspective for the man, his head
at the scale of touch, unmoved
from the pillow, as if he's drifting
on a cloud, ready
                    for the zoom to skin,
the back of his hand, an intimate map
of 10 square centimeters, landscape
of creases and crevices breaking apart
to the microscope's probe, tissue
like canyon walls.
                    As if to surprise,
the sudden blossom of a giant
white blood cell—ruffled anemone
afloat in the current of the body,
in *a hundred times more cells*
than stars in the Galaxy—
                    and my feeling
lost, at 10^{-7} meters, in the deep dark
nucleus, enormous molecules—coiled
DNA—a few centimeters long,
message spelled out in twisted ladders,
abacus beads, carbon and hydrogen,
elements of the stars.
                    As if the surface
of one atom, haze of electrons
in motion, purposely mimics a night sky
to rocket through—four pages' worth—
before arrival at the protons and neutrons,
tight clustered moons a bit smaller
than billiard balls,
                    whose insides
must be imagined, as if it all reduces
down to searching harder, deeper,

to the longing that it matter, powerful
quarks in their high-speed dance,
a painted heaven at 10^{-15} meters,
multicolored spots, symmetrical
yet untrackable, at the end
$$\text{of the book.}$$

just made for parties, I suppose, our host, Dave, breaking up
the corners of laughter, corralling us in front of the fireplace.

*If you could choose, would you rather have the power
of invisibility or flight?* The sudden ticking clock meant we

good guests were mulling over options, striving to be right
or clever, except for Sara and Melanie who weren't afraid

to shout *Flight!* and *Me too!*, eager to get back to food, wine, a little
flirting, unlike their husbands, Bruce and Pete, preferring the
fantasy

of the question to the fantasy of the party (everyone dressed up
and aglow), delving into *invisibility,* the chance to spy

on their *boss meeting with his boss* or on *stock market insiders,*
to linger *in the middle of a women's locker room,* ideas exposing

the practical among us—*Would our clothes be invisible too?
Could we carry food, a cell phone? Not get run over?*

And can the whole invisibility thing be turned off and on at will?
Dave, resolved into a mute observer, sat grinning, shrugging

even when Roger persisted—*No informed decision
can be made without knowing if we would be invisible to radar*

*and heat signatures. Also, if light passes right through you,
it wouldn't hit your retinas, thus rendering you blind. Clearly,*

flying is the logical choice. Bruce wasn't about to give up
on that locker room—*How fast and how far can one fly?*

What about bird strikes? Or being sucked into jet engines?
Besides, if I were invisible, I could board any plane I wanted to.

Sara rolled her eyes—*The point of flying, my dear, isn't to get*
somewhere, but to soar, to be free, to see the world anew—

and Marcie sighed, *Being short is almost like being invisible.*
So is getting old, said Tom, *even when you're six feet tall.*

Sad, how locker rooms and diamond heists didn't occur to me,
how I only thought about tickling or kicking a politician

while he's on TV, about cleaning my gutters by floating. Guess
I'd like both powers. Roger started in with his tsk-tsking noises—

Well, if we're going to break the rules, and dream, then I want
useful powers—ESP, the strength of Hercules, teleportation.

Rather than telling him where he could teleport to,
I said, *I've never had one of those dreams where I fly.*

The whole room *oh*'d, pity instantly signing me up:
Flying. Imagine, not ever having to worry about falling

or rush hour, and maybe flight could somehow burn calories too.
Dave jumped up, swung his empty glass, his slurring words—

You're all missing the point, and I can't believe anyone
who claims to pick flying because deep down everyone longs

to be invisible, to figure out what people are really like,
like when they're alone, like my ex for instance, except she's not

*alone anymore, and—*And Tom put his arm around Dave's shoulder,
said, *I know exactly what you mean. Don't you think it might be best*

to have neither power, both with so many damn responsibilities,
and don't we already have enough of those? Dave nodded,

as we did, grateful to carry our plates to the kitchen,
to the immutable apple pie and coffee we knew how

to savor—like Dave's bear hugs, later at the door, where he stood
a bit teary-eyed, guiding our arms into heavy, wingless coats.

V.

The house is a bird's very person; it is its form and its most immediate effort, I shall even say, its suffering . . . There is not one of these blades of grass that in order to make it curve and hold the curve, has not been pressed on countless times by the bird's breast, its heart . . .

JULES MICHELET

The woman next to me says she's going home—
    emphatically, in that tenor of youth—
        to Tuscaloosa, to introduce

her six-month-old son to his grandparents,
    two connecting flights away.
        On both of our small screens,

a figure of the plane blinks from the black
    dot of *Frankfurt* toward the dot
        labeled *Detroit,* everyone

facing some definite *B,* backs turned
    to this morning's overcast *A.*
        The baby squirms when she adds

We live on a base in Germany.
    My husband is being redeployed
        to Iraq. Nothing I can do but pray.

The war is more than two years long and I've
    never met a soldier who's served there
        or the family of such a soldier, until now,

in this assigned aisle seat, where I answer
    I'm on my way home too. I was
        in Germany with my dad on vacation.

I don't explain about hidden layers
    under the map of Poland, the farm
        that had been my great-grandfather's,

how we visited there also, all the German
    headstones gone, toppled after World War II.
        As her baby drinks another bottle,

she fills out the customs form, and wonders
    aloud if her place of residency
        is Germany or the United States.

In front of us, a woman wears a burka.
    What is the view like, cut and hemmed
        into fabric, a tiny window to the world?

The baby's bright eyes look everywhere
    as I hold and bounce the soft heft of him,
        his mother in line for the restroom,

the flight almost over. I look across the aisle
    at my father and think of the canal
        he showed me, where he'd splashed

as a child, how war and the Oder River
    charted his life. Dad smiles at me, the baby,
        leans over to sing a German lullaby,

the baby tired, as we all are, of tray tables
    and screens, countless tiny points. Let *B*
        be the place called making a baby happy.

You be this guy, my two-year-old nephew
says once more, unaware he's discovered
sentences and what a pushover
I am for his big, eager eyes,
the way he presses the Playmobil man
into my hand. For what must be
the twentieth time now, Henry flies
his bright red helicopter
through the sunshine of the room
while I find my spot for distress—
the swamp of the rug or the cliff
of the couch. He doesn't rescue me
right away, waits for my calls
of *Help! Help!,* the detailed pleas:
My leg is broken! or *An alligator
is coming!* Henry pretends he doesn't
hear me, laughs when I plead harder—
Oh, please, please hurry!
The alligator is getting close!
Finally, overcome by empathy
or suspense, he runs to me
in full waddle-zoom, stalling
the copter into hover, intent
on watching my fingers push
the plastic figure up the swinging ladder,
through the little window.
You sit here! You sit here! he chants
and points yet again, as if I might forget
he's the guy in the pilot seat
and that I need to bend just so
in order to mold to the cockpit,
shouting *Thank you!* as he carries me away.

Upon Being Asked What I Believe In

I say, for starters, the word *in*,
the way it dumps quicksand before
love and *trouble*, or after *belief*
and *jump right!* I say the days I'm sunk
in up to my waist, improvising
with ingredients at hand. I say the sizzle
of bacon, onions, the wooden spoon
meandering through thick lentil soup
with basil. I say all the herbs in my garden,
pushing roots into earth. I say the Zen
of weeding, aches that follow. And how,
in Japan, they seat a guest facing away
from the most beautiful part of the room,
remember the person later as what's missing
from the art. I say my first slow dance,
the texture of polyester against my cheek,
those hit songs I wrote out, cataloged.
I say catalogs, glossy paper, the thrill
of promises, anticipation. I say afternoon naps,
dark chocolate, gin martinis. And wine,
the best I ever tasted from a styrofoam cup,
the nurse urging me to gulp it down
my second day of labor. I say my babies'
milk-drunk faces. And my teenage sons,
the way they answer me in French, pleased
that I can't understand. I almost talk about being
the only woman in the house. I say, whatever
Lisa Simpson believes in. And, yes, the saxophone.
I say music from unexpected sources,
the younger me sent to test cars
in 30°-below Fairbanks, how I let a local
drive me away from town one midnight for a chance
at the aurora borealis, how I shivered
from the colors. I say the starkness of snow

on a wheat field or in the backyard, deep drifts
obscuring the picnic table, my tears. I say the weight
of twilight, moonrise, voices that drift
through the living room: Louis Armstrong,
Eudora Welty, my husband offering
to warm my feet. I say sharing the thermostat
and the covers and the Sunday *Times.* I say the pulse
of algebra, all those x's busy intersecting
all those y's, points aligned. I say the tangle
of science and poetry, *earthworm*
and *wormhole,* the tunneling mind. And the wild
flight of fireflies, bodies glowing
from both desire and defense.

Harder than it used to be—climbing the rungs,
   up and down pressure of my cloth along the glass,
      thoughts of my father, his anger on the phone
         today after his physical, his new doctor treating him

like a four-year-old instead of a seventy-four-year-old,
   asking, *Do you have any trouble going poop?*
      of a man who's read Schiller and Tolstoy, Twain
         and Hawkins, but speaks what he, himself, calls *broken*

English, carries union insurance, calloused hands,
   backache from decades of lifting bricks and blocks.
      When my father washes windows, cuts his grass,
         cooks his dinner, he whistles or hums or sings—

that is, he always did. Strange, to be unsure now.
   Strange, his face a splash older each time I visit,
      the glimpse of my reflection—and his—in this pane,
         of the blonde-haired girl of five, *Papa* teaching me

to recite German poetry, *langsam und laut* (slow and loud).
   When I gave my first poetry reading, at forty, he drove through
      rush hour, sat in the front row, recognized the building:
         I worked on this YMCA around the time you were born.

Now, in afternoon sun, I stretch toward out-of-reach corners,
   a stubborn teenage memory—my father's birthday,
      his eyes weepy from drink, the two of us in the kitchen
         past midnight, his sighs over *Schlesien* (Silesia),

Land der Dichter (land of the poets), his watery words
   about generations to follow—*Maybe someday*
      we'll have a writer in the family again,
         the smack of what he didn't say—*Maybe you.*

Each window just leads to the next, to something
 I've said or left unsaid. *Perhaps the doctor talks*
  to everyone like that, I offered, but he didn't buy it,
   just as he hadn't bought the doctor's pitch for yet another

drug, one to *keep your bones strong* which, *yes, I suppose*
 could result in more kidney stones—the doctor angry too,
  scribbling as he muttered, *If you refuse the medicine,*
   I'm forced to document it was your decision.

How little, really, we decide in life, how wild the impact,
 what gets learned by heart . . . *Der Purpur gleitet, gleitet*
  I say aloud, shocked at the sudden ring of accent,
   my first language neglected, the tongue a muscle too,

sorrow unraveling from the translation (the regal cloak
 is sliding, sliding), from the weave of Dad's voice
  eager to tell me other news—this morning
   his willow tree studded with blackbirds, their caws

drawing him outside, how he knew *they were crying*
 a warning. I didn't know birds gathered like that
  for a reason, couldn't guess I'd replay his scene
   the way I reread poems or double-check windows

for shine, for spots I might have missed—
 his careful tiptoeing behind the shed, how he watched
  and waited, the size of the owl, span and pump
   of the wings taking his breath away, even as he talked.

On Art

Everybody discusses and pretends
to understand . . . when it is simply
necessary to love.

CLAUDE MONET

The Magpie outsells all the other postcards
    at the Musée d'Orsay: sunlit snow,
        a hope-yellow sky, lone bird on a fence.

Did Monet see a magpie or create one,
    the landscape needing a heartbeat
        or the other way around?

I want a postcard of the man I watched
    this morning, my heart pounding
        as he stood treestill on the trail,

arms outstretched, feeding birds
    from his palms. Blink-quick, a chickadee
        lit, then soared, seed in its beak,

body disappearing into pines.
    How to remember the pinch of tiny claws,
        the flutter of something wild?

I've read that art is about afterthought—
    the magpie and the moments that follow,
        empty fence, shifting shadows—

and wonder if love, too, is art,
    because we crave its thrill,
        emotion swooping down on wings,

feathers gleaming in the sun,
    until the slightest movement,
        the briefest doubt, changes their hue.

To My Mother, on Her Wedding Day

Already, photos arrive on my computer—you
in bronze brocade and lace, Gerhard with a rose

boutonniere, the two of you blushing after a dozen years
of morning *Kaffee,* evening *Brot,* countless German

potatoes, and those golden pears you've learned
to grow and cook and can together. I recognize

all the relatives in the room and that certain smile
of yours making me smile back, across the ocean.

I can almost smell your perfume, hear your voice
as on the phone: *A trumpet played . . . We lit a candle . . .*

The day was perfect, except my daughters weren't here.
Here, the first time around—an impulsive 1957 Monday

in Detroit, Dad rained out from the job site—your only
witness had been a burly cop. Almost fifty years later,

Gerhard's grandchildren gave you an American touch—
clanking cans and a *Just Married* sign fastened to your car.

I think of how Gerhard's son had chuckled at your plan,
asking *Why marry now?* and of all those other questions,

forms, visits to the U.S. consulate and a German judge.
You said, *We have to prove who we are.*

In your first job, at eighteen, you were a green-
carded waitress, all starch and apron, carrying a silver tray

at parties for Grosse Pointe debutantes. *Cheers!*
I say—and *Prost!*—to your own dance, at last,

to your sparkling champagne and face filling my screen—
life-size wrinkles, joy—leaving only the merest margin

for worry (his insulin, your lithium . . .). How good that today
is not a new beginning, another arrival or departure.

Just married.

Our Twenty-First Summer, Chimney Swifts

1.

You didn't believe me
when I said I heard birds
through the fireplace doors.

Twittering, twittering, twittering.

The next time you mowed
you came in smiling—
Birds flew from the chimney.
They dove over and over
right in front of the tractor.

Sustenance snapped up
from tiny flutters.

2.

And this is why I love you—
because you looked the birds up,
told me they're endangered.

I need to wait for fall before I can
put back the chimney cap.

Not enough hollow trees around.
Maybe next year I should build
a wooden nesting tower.

3.

I dreamt two swifts were flying
in our bedroom as we slept.

They were weaving a pattern
I could and couldn't figure out.

The clock was gone.

I felt your breath on my shoulder.

There was no need
to wake.

4.

Funny, about swifts.

Not built to perch, they can't land
in the grass or on a branch.

They live mostly in the air,
even mating on the wing.

A wingspan more than
twice as long as their bodies—
silhouette of tiny arrow
and wide-reaching bow.

Erratic flight—shallow beats,
sudden stalls, startling speed.

5.

So here we are again—or still—
in our living room,
the sound of chirping,
incessant twilight hunger.

Your hand in mine,
we talk of our sons
growing older.

Impulse, to break off twigs
in passing, to keep on
gluing the nest together.

A half-saucer nest is enough.

Night allows some rest,
clawed feet clamped side by side,
firebricks with mortared joints—
a cliff wall to cling to.

May 2005

"Not another bird poem," I tell myself, as I keep
making notes from Birding Babylon,
the web log of a U.S. soldier in Iraq.

> *The crested lark, one of the most common birds here.*
> *They run a few feet, stop and look around,*
> *repeat this all day long.*

Two days ago my oldest son turned eighteen,
and already, in the mail, the Selective Service
registration form: "It's quick, it's easy,
and it's the law" in bold above a stoic eagle,
cartoon-style, huge muscle-builder arms
folded in defiance.

> *Clouds of sand rolling through.*
> *A broken wood pigeon egg at the base of a tamarisk tree,*
> *the pigeon still sitting on the nest.*

Defiant, too, it turns out, the ivory-billed woodpecker
and all who didn't stop searching
sixty years after the bird was deemed extinct.
In the grocery store and bagel shop, I've heard
conversations about the sighting, the video.
No one talks about the war, new bombings
reported every morning.

> *A lot of rocket and mortar attacks.*
> *We go everywhere in body armor and helmet.*
> *A day for birding in "full battle rattle."*

What good all the rattling—
the blog, the news, eyewitness and breaking.

Sixty years ago, victorious, giant headlines.
Today, "Parade of Troops Celebrate
in Moscow," while, much further down,
"The exercise of Communism has killed
over 80 million people in Europe and Asia."

Flew in and around Mosul.
Huge numbers of birds in the Tigris.
We were moving too fast to get a good look.

Click. Click. Click. Links on my screen
lead to French scientists waiting for the swallows
to arrive, to announce another spring,
but the birds are missing, their numbers "decreasing 87%
in the last 13 years," which makes me think
of a thirteen-year-old I know who says, when he grows up,
he's going to be a sniper.

Wood pigeons everywhere.
They power up at a 45 degree angle, then swoop down,
flight path in the shape of a sine wave,
almost like they're doing it for fun.

I suppose it must be fun—the boy
and all kinds of people playing online
world games, battling computer-controlled monsters
and each other. Why else would they spend
$800 million a year on "virtual add-ins"—
$300 for "Boots of the Storm"
or $625 for a "Black-Plated Neck Collar"—
buying more strength for their animated character.

On our convoy one of the Humvees had a flat.
We set up a defensive perimeter
with our weapons pointing out.
Ten feet from me, a pair of crested larks,
the male dancing, displaying.

Displayed for me: "ACTION ALERT!
HQ CALLING CHRISTINE RHEIN!"
on the cover of *The Military Book Club* catalog,
and inside—"This Season's Best . . . A Brand New
Take on Wars . . . Tank Girls: In and Out
of Uniform . . . The Sexy Side of Soldiering."

As I was watching some wood pigeons
a pair of F-16s came tearing down the runway,
afterburners going, the noise incredible,
the birds unfazed.

On the radio this week I listened
to the author of *Why Birds Sing*—
"Because they must," he said, "and because they love to"—
his clarinet recorded in an Australian rainforest,
a wild lyrebird joining the improvisation,
the give and take and abandon,
music titled "Pillow of Air."

Mission in the desert.
A crested lark hovering 100 feet off the ground
singing its heart out.

So why not write about the strawberry finches
building a nest outside my front window,
the way one of them—burden of a long, complicated twig
in its beak—tried to find a big enough entrance,
dense needles blocking each effort, the finch
ramming the twig and itself against the branches
over and over, until it slipped deep into the green,
the bush quivering from the work of weaving.

Near an amphitheater from Alexander the Great's time,
a black-crowned night heron, a few little egrets . . .
my first laughing dove.

NOTES

"Imagining Her Letter" and "One of those questions" were both inspired by segments of *This American Life*, the Chicago Public Radio program.

"Upon Being Asked What I Believe In" is modeled after Dean Young's poem, "On Being Asked by a Student If He Should Ask Out Some Girl."

Italicized sections of the poem "Not Another" are adapted, with the author's permission, from the online birding journal of National Guardsman Sergeant First Class Jonathan Trouern-Trend during his tour of duty with the 118th Area Support Medical Battalion in Iraq. Highlights from Trouern-Trend's web log are collected in a book, *Birding Babylon*.

Selected by Robert A. Fink, *Wild Flight* is the seventeenth winner of the Walt McDonald First-Book Competition in Poetry. The competition is supported generously through donated subscriptions from *The American Scholar, The Atlantic Monthly, The Georgia Review, Gulf Coast, The Hudson Review, The Massachusetts Review, Poetry, Shenandoah*, and *The Southern Review*.